FOR SNORRI

X

First published 2016 by Two Hoots

This edition published 2019 by Two Hoots

an imprint of Pan Macmillan

20 New Wharf Road, London N1 9RR

Associated companies throughout the world

www.panmacmillan.com

ISBN: 978-1-5098-3144-9

Text and illustrations © Morag Hood 2016, 2019

Moral rights asserted.

1 3 5 7 9 8 6 4 2

A CIP catalogue record for this book is available from the British Library.

Printed in China

The illustrations in this book were created using supermarket carrier bags.

www.twohootsbooks.com

MORAG HOOD

Colin and Lee
Carrot and Pea

TWO HOOTS

This is Lee.

He is a pea.

All of his friends are peas.

Except Colin.

Colin isn't a pea.

He is much too tall
to be a pea,

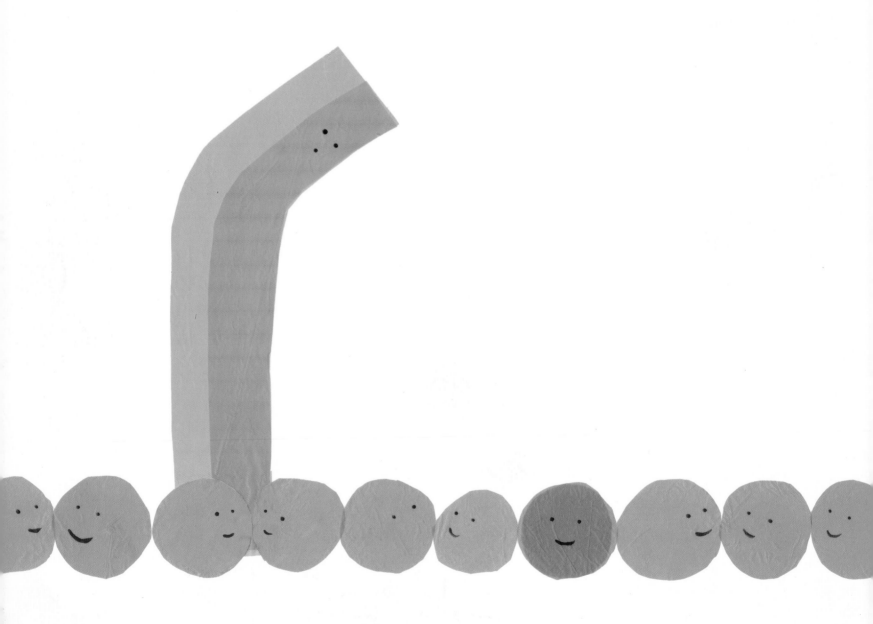

and very orange.

He can't roll like a pea,

or bounce like a pea.

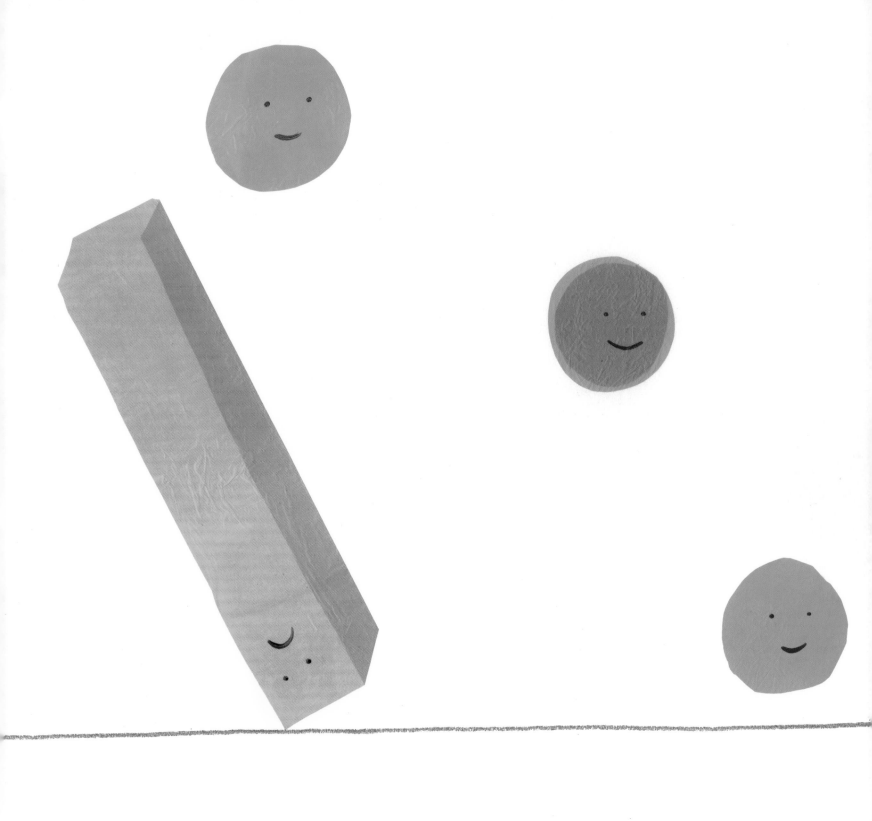

And he isn't very good at playing hide-and-seek.

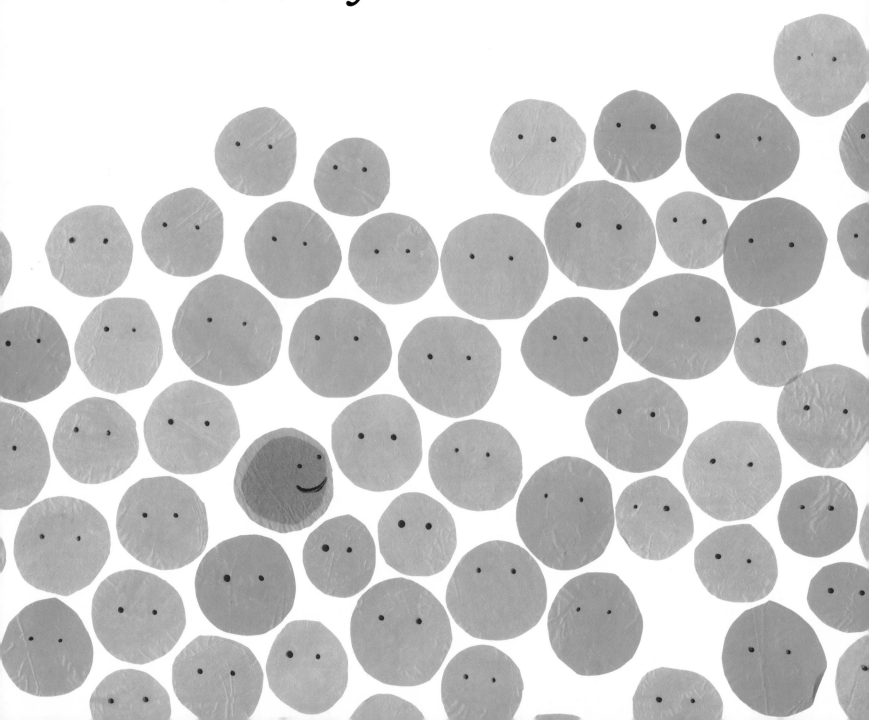

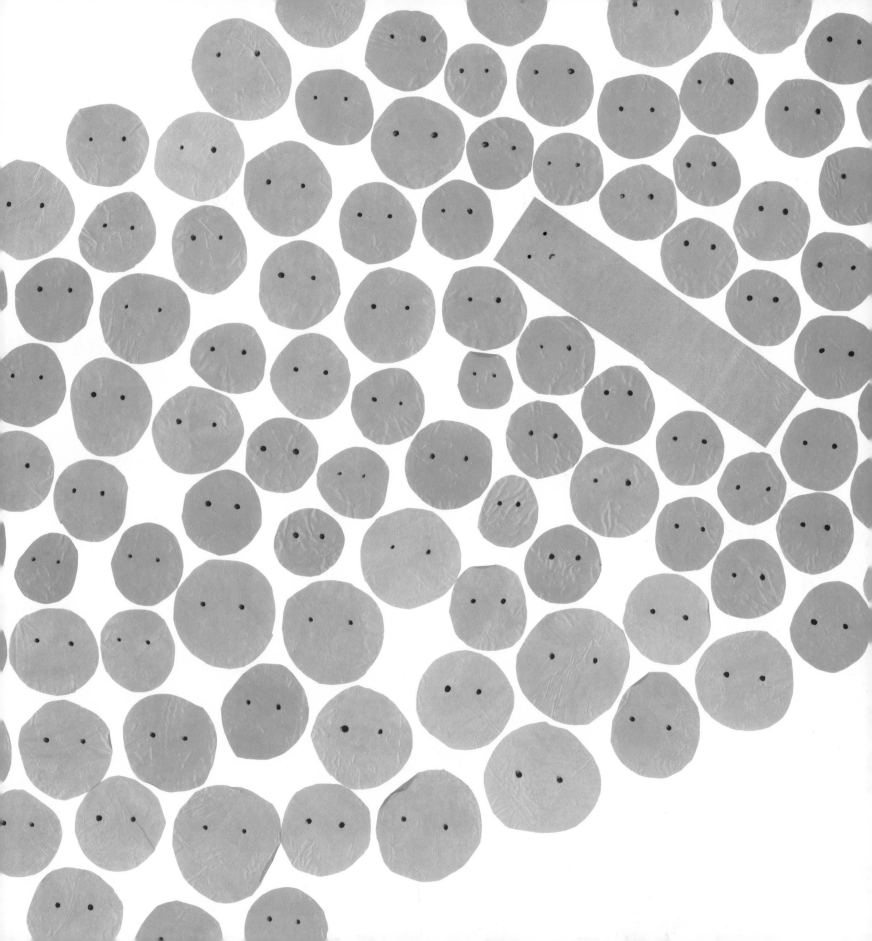

But Colin makes an
excellent tower,

a fantastic bridge,

and a great slide.

Colin isn't at all like Lee
and the other peas,

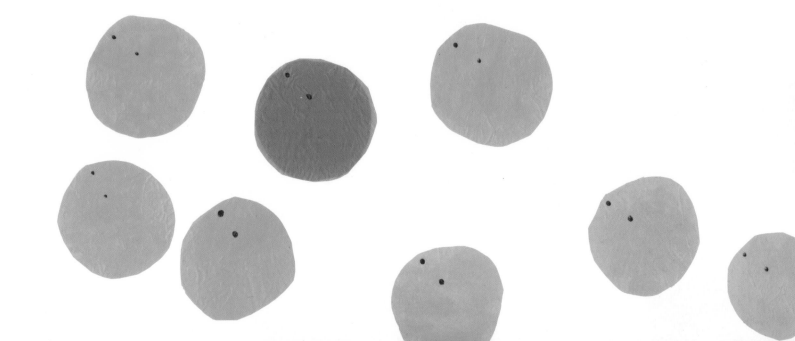

but they are
the best of friends.

Morag Hood loves thinking of different ways to tell stories and make pictures. Morag made Colin and Lee and the other peas by cutting out shapes from old supermarket plastic bags and sticking them on paper.

What fun things could you use to make your own pictures? Remember to get a grown up to help you!

CONTENTS

BASIC SHAPES

The craft ideas in this book have all been made with coloured modelling clay. You can also use air dry clays that you paint later. It's up to you, but whatever you choose... have fun!

Tools you may need:

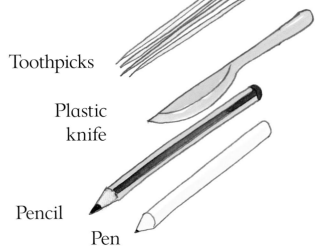

Toothpicks

Plastic knife

Pencil

Pen

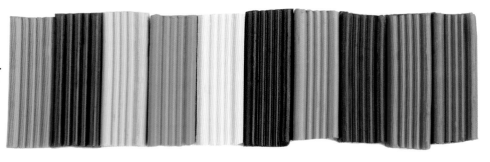

You will need a rainbow of clay! (Or paints if you plan to use air dry clays.)

To make a ball, roll the clay in the palm of your hand until it's round.

To make a tear shape, roll one end of the ball into a point.

To make a long sausage or cylinder shape, roll clay backward and forward on a flat surface.

4

CLAY
ARTY Crafty

SCRIBBLERS

WITH SIMPLE STEP-BY-STEP INSTRUCTIONS

Mark

Published in Great Britain in MMXIX by
Scribblers, an imprint of
The Salariya Book Company Ltd
25 Marlborough Place,
Brighton BN1 1UB
www.salariya.com

SALARIYA
SCRIBO BOOK HOUSE SCRIBBLERS

© The Salariya Book Company Ltd MMXIX

ISBN-13: 978-1-912537-00-6

1 3 5 7 9 8 6 4 2

A CIP catalogue record for this book
is available from the British Library.

Printed and bound in China.

Printed on paper from sustainable sources.

Visit
www.salariya.com
for our online catalogue and
free fun stuff.

To cut sharp edges, use a plastic knife or a strong piece of card.

To make a disc, flatten a ball of clay with the palm of your hand.

To attach a piece of clay, gently push it into the surface with your fingertips.

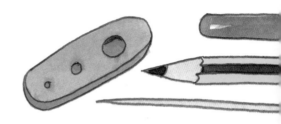

To make different size indents in the clay, try using the ends of different tools.

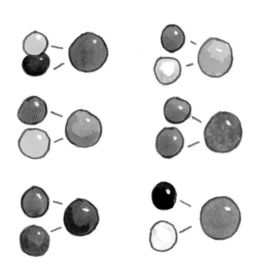

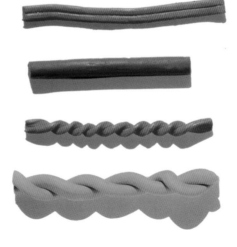

This shows you how to make new colours. Mix two colours together until they make a new colour, i.e. yellow + blue = green.

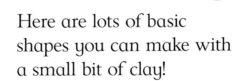

Here are lots of basic shapes you can make with a small bit of clay!

5

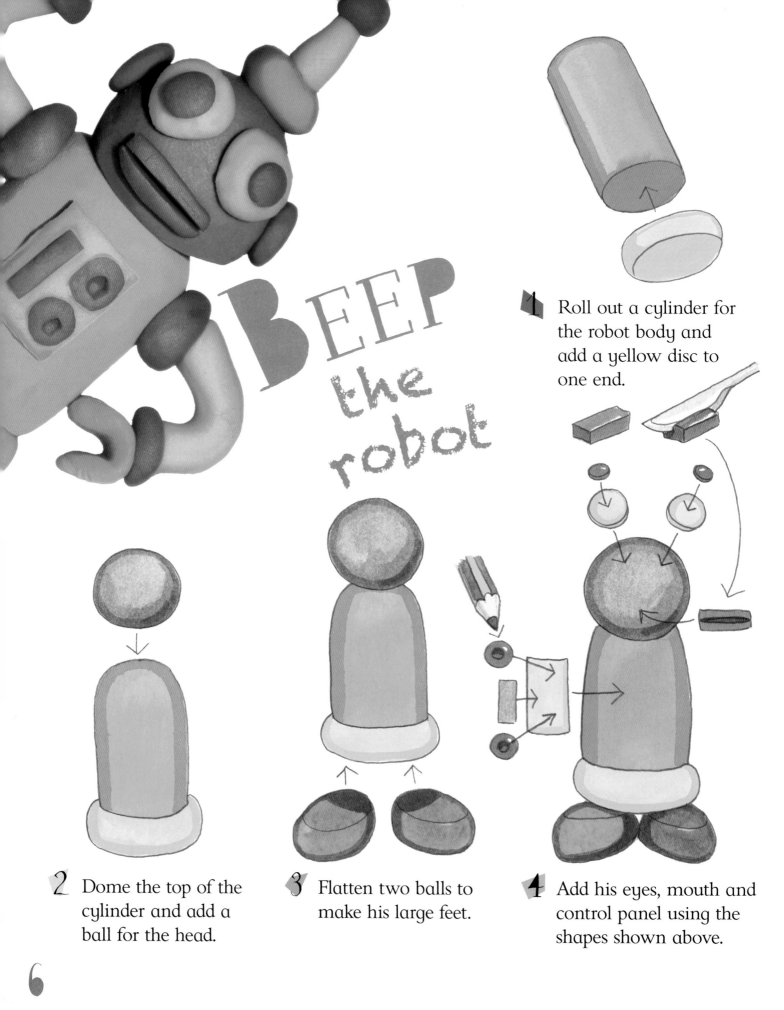

BEEP the robot

1 Roll out a cylinder for the robot body and add a yellow disc to one end.

2 Dome the top of the cylinder and add a ball for the head.

3 Flatten two balls to make his large feet.

4 Add his eyes, mouth and control panel using the shapes shown above.

6 Each arm is made out of four pieces of clay (as shown above).

5 Add two ears. Make his antenna out of three pieces of clay.

7 Join the arms to the sides of his body.

Beep!

Beep!

Boop!

NORMAN
the sheep

1 Roll out all these parts and lots of balls for the woolly coat (right).

2 Join the sausage-shaped legs to the body.

3 Add the oval-shaped head and two flat ears. Use a toothpick to attach his head.

4 Indent the nostrils with a pencil point and attach discs for the eyes.

5 Finish off his eyes with two small black balls and add a little tail.

6 Add lots of white balls to make his woolly coat.

Baaa! Baaa!

GREEN TREE

1 Roll out a cone shape. Cut the end off so the base is flat.

2 Make a small cylinder for the tree trunk.

3 Join the cone to the cylinder using a toothpick.

4 Roll out lots of small balls. Use your fingers to roll out one end to make them tear-shaped.

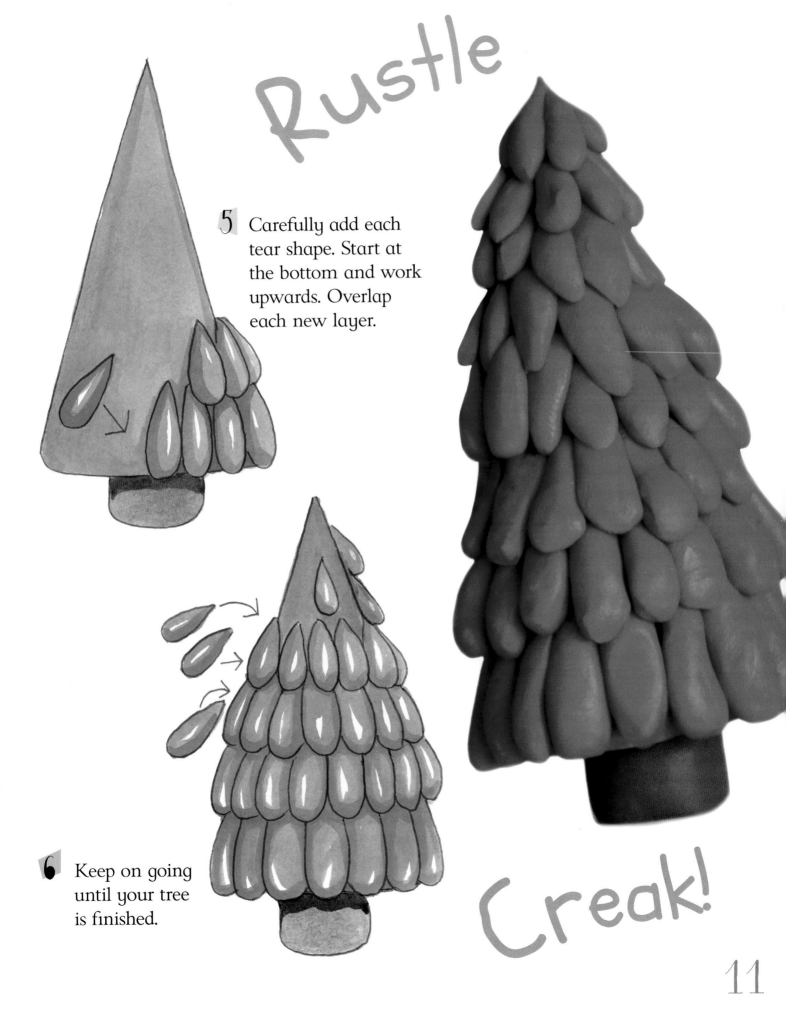

Rustle

5 Carefully add each tear shape. Start at the bottom and work upwards. Overlap each new layer.

6 Keep on going until your tree is finished.

Creak!

11

M●LLY the cat

Puuuurrrr!

Stripes

Body

Ears

Face

Tail

Head

Legs

1 Make all the shapes shown above. Use orange, brown, pink, white and black clay.

2 Fix the cat's head onto her body. Use a toothpick.

3 Attach her legs and make sure she can stand!

4 Attach her long curly tail.

12

5 Add two white discs for the eyes, and an orange snout shape.

6 Attach both ears and a black nose. Indent with a pencil (as shown).

7 Add stripes, a pink tongue and black dots on the eyes.

8 Use the remaining brown strips for her stripy coat.

Meow!

Meow!

13

Attention!

TIM the soldier

1 Make these shapes (above) out of red, blue, black, white and pink clay.

2 Use a plastic knife to carve out the soldier's legs and feet shape.

3 Join the feet, legs, body, neck and head using toothpicks.

4 Now add his big black hat.

14

Sir!

5 The arms are made from three pieces, fixed close to his body. Add a red plume to his hat.

6 Make little eyes, ears, a nose and whiskers. Add a yellow hat strap.

7 Cut two white strips and cross them over his body.

15

BILL
the penguin

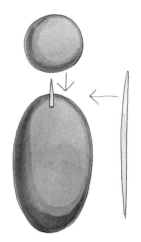

1 Join the head to an oval for the body using a toothpick.

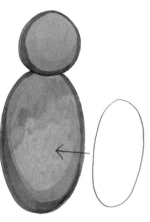

2 Make a flat oval out of white clay. Fix it onto his tummy.

3 Flatten two orange balls into discs for his feet. Attach (as shown).

4 Make two flat ovals for his wings. Attach to the body.

5 Add eyes using discs and black dots.

6 The beak: roll out a flat orange disc. Now fold in half. Make the fold curved so it will fit onto the penguin's round head.

Honk!
Honk!

7 Now bend one wing
up so Bill is waving.

17

FRANCINE the bear

Grrrrr!
Grrrrr!

1 Join the bear's head and body using a toothpick.

2 Roll and cut two cylinders. Attach legs.

3 Add a tear-shaped arm to each side.

4 Attach her ears and her snout.

18

5 Make her eyes, nose and mouth. Attach (as shown).

Growl!!

6 Finish off by adding flat pads to her tummy, paws and ears.

19

FORMULA 1
racing car

1 Make a long rectangle and cut one end at an angle (as shown).

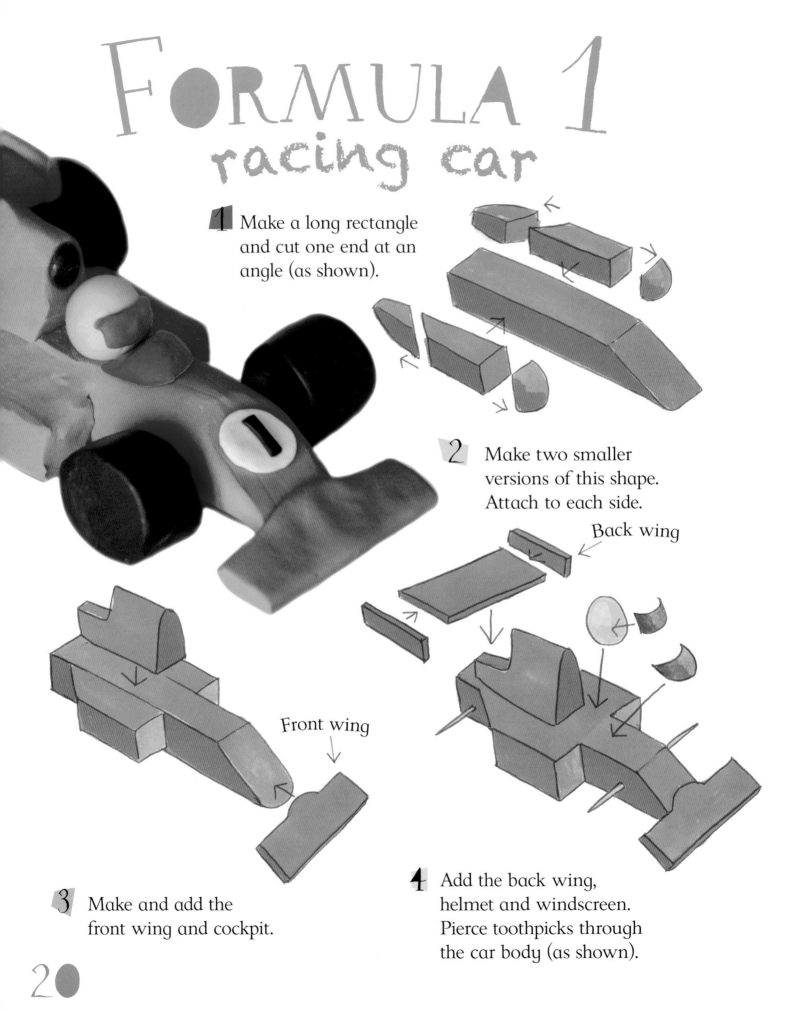

2 Make two smaller versions of this shape. Attach to each side.

Back wing

3 Make and add the front wing and cockpit.

Front wing

4 Add the back wing, helmet and windscreen. Pierce toothpicks through the car body (as shown).

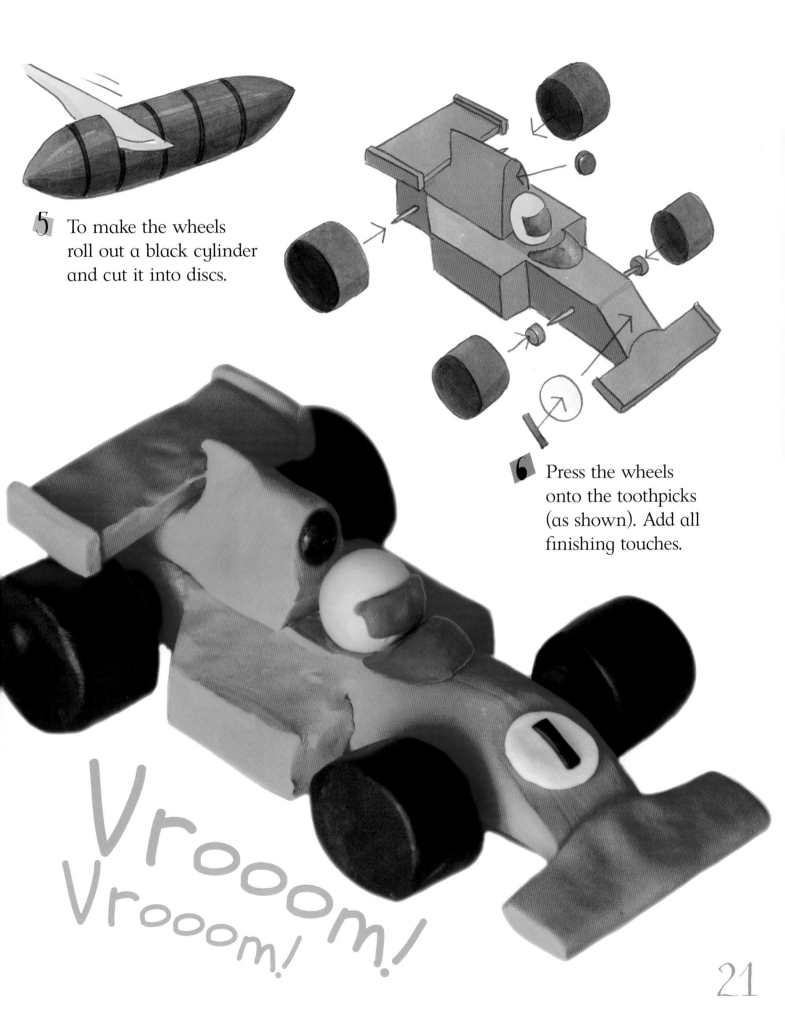

5 To make the wheels roll out a black cylinder and cut it into discs.

6 Press the wheels onto the toothpicks (as shown). Add all finishing touches.

Vrooom! Vrooom!

21

JACK
o'Lantern
Wooooooooo!

1 Roll out a big orange ball.

2 Squish it down into a pumpkin shape.

3 Use your thumb to indent the top.

4 Using a plastic knife, cut deep grooves into your pumpkin.

5 Roll out and mould a green stalk.

6 Flatten and roll out some black clay.

7 Now use a plastic knife to cut out the eyes, nose and mouth (as shown).

8 Press these shapes onto your pumpkin.

Boo!

23

Sven

the
snowman

Brrr!

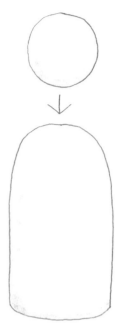

1 Roll a ball into a long shape for the snowman's body. Cut off the bottom to flatten it. Now attach a ball for the head.

2 Roll two sausage shapes for the arms. Attach on each side.

3 Roll a green cylinder shape. Cut and flatten a piece to wrap around his neck.

4 Cut two more bits for the rest of his scarf. Add a ball for the knot.

24

5 Indent his mouth with a toothpick. Add black balls for eyes and a red cone for his nose.

6 Add two black balls for buttons.

7 Make Sven's hat with a flat black disc with a cylinder on top.

Brrr!

Brrr!

JET plane

Zoom!

1 Make a flattish square shape. Make a long rectangle and cut the front at an angle (as shown). Now join the shapes together.

Canopy

2 Roll and flatten some clay to cut out the wing shape. Then make the canopy. Attach both.

3 Cut out two slim rectangles. Place behind the wings.

Rear wing

4 Cut out two black squares for the air intakes. Cut the small rear wings and attach.

5 Cut the engine exhausts from orange cylinders and the wheels from blue.

6 Roll out a long sausage of yellow clay. Flatten it to add yellow strips.

Zoom!

Bob
the
meerkat

Hi!

1 Roll a long sausage shape out. Round off one end and cut a flat base.

2 Roll a ball for the head. Join it to the body using a toothpick.

3 Make a long, flat oval for the tummy. Cut out both feet shapes and attach.

4 Make long, flat tear-shaped arms. Attach.

5 Attach two flat orange discs to his head.

6 Add the eyes: a black disc, then a white disc, then another black.

28

7 Make a snout shape. Add a ball for the nose. Indent his mouth with a pencil.

8 Attach his ear shapes with black semi-circles inside.

9 Add pads to his paws.

Hi!

MADDY
the owl
Hoot! Hoot!

1 Make a ball of clay for the body and squish it into a disc shape.

2 Add two big white discs for her eyes.

3 Cut and attach some flat orange clay for her breast.

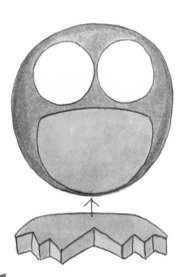

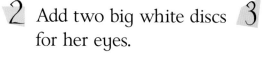

4 Cut out her feet and toes (as shown) and attach to the body.

5 Finish off her eyes with two small black balls. Add her beak shape.

6 Mould two small ears to add to her head.

7 Roll out three tubes. Squeeze together. Cut off the ends and halve it to make two wings.

8 Add a wing to each side of her body.

Hoot!

Hoot!

Hoot!

Hoot!

31

GLOSSARY

Antenna a rod-shaped object that can pick up electrical signals.

Base the bottom of something, such as a shape or object.

Canopy In an aircraft, the canopy is the see-through bit that covers the cockpit where the pilot sits.

Cone a shape with a circular base at one end and a point at the other.

Cylinder a long shape with circular ends.

Indent a dip or hole made in something by pressing into it.

Plume a feather or collection of feathers worn on the head as decoration.

Toothpick A thin wooden stick with a pointed end that can be used to cut shapes into clay.

INDEX